Out of the Underworld

Poems by Patricia Nelson

ALSO BY PATRICIA NELSON

Among the Shapes that Fold & Fly, Sugartown Publishing, 2013
Spokes of Dream or Bird, Poetic Matrix Press, 2017

COVER ART BY SAUNDRA KIEHN

Poetic Matrix Press
www.poeticmatrix.com

ACKNOWLEDGMENTS

Grateful acknowledgement is made to the following publications in which these poems first appeared or in which first periodical publication is pending, sometimes in a slightly different form.

"December Daylight" in *Panoplyzine*, Spring 2017
"Cezanne" in *Panoplyzine*, Summer/Fall 2017
"Light that Purifies" and "Out of the Underworld" in *2RiverView,* Fall 2017
"Another Massacre and Driving Home" in *Panoplyzine*, Winter 2018
"The Lovers" in *Blue Unicorn*, February 2018
"Brigid," "The Loved," and "The Mountain Roars" in OUT OF SILENCE . . . AND THEN (Redwood Writers Poetry Anthology 2018, Eds. Claggett & Bernstein)
"Bear and Devil" in *Illuminations*, 2018
"Breugel" in Breugel/Bosch Ekphrastic Anthology (Ed. David A. Sullivan, forthcoming, exact title TBD)
"Nub on the Axe of the World" in REVERBERATIONS: A VISUAL CONVERSATION (Ed. Charles Prendergast, 2018)
"Daphne" in the Sitting Room Anthology 2018
"Empty" in the Marin Poetry Center Anthology 2018
"Gate" in *California Quarterly*, Summer 2018
"Symbolic Animals" in *The Listening Eye*, 2018
"What Came Before Exile" and "Something Half-Seen" in *Hubbub*, Fall 2018
"Anastasia" in *Panoplyzine*, Fall 2018
"Crazy Otto" in *Califragile*, October 2018
"Fire" in *Blue Unicorn*, Fall 2018
"Where the Oldest Gods Lived" in *Califragile*, November 2018
"Amelia Earhart" in *Rockvale Review*, Fall 2018
"Goat's Eye" in *Algebra of Owls*, November 2018
"Smoke" in *Califragile*, December 2018

"Dark" in *Algebra of Owls*, December 2018
"Hanging Man," "Clean," and "Prayers of Intercession" in *American Journal of Poetry*, January 2019
"Then I Was Here" in *Pangolin Review*, January 2019
"The Rivers" in *Loch Raven Review,* Spring 2019
"Star," "Believer's Candle," "Narcissus," "Siren Searching," and "Night in Purgatory" in CROW: IN THE LIGHT OF DAY, IN THE DARK OF NIGHT (Redwood Writers Poetry Anthology 2019, Eds. Fran Claggett & Les Bernstein)
"Magician" in *Pangolin Review,* March 2019
"Nasturtium" in *California Quarterly*, Spring 2019
"Climbing at Night" in *Porter Gulch Literary & Arts Review,* 2019
"Almost There" in *River Poets Journal,* April 2019 (National Poetry Month collection of pocket poems)
"Sunflowers" in *Pangolin Review,* July 2019
"Explorer," "Oedipus," "Death Card," and "Easter Island Heads" in *Academy of the Heart and Mind,* Summer 2019
"Moment" in *Eunoia Review,* August 2019
"High Priestess" in *Califragile*, August 2019
"Persephone" in *Blue Unicorn,* Fall 2019
"Sofia" and "The Line" in *Willawaw Journal,* Fall 2019

Contents

Out of the Underworld

Exile Monologues

Your Eye's Blue and Wishing Moth

OTHERWORLD

PURGATORY (AFTER DANTE)

THIRST FOR LIGHT

ABOUT THE AUTHOR

DEDICATION

With thanks and fondness for all of the poets with
whom I have worked and studied; for poetry
mentors Fran Claggett and Terry Ehret; and most
particularly for the remarkable Hart family, which
set me on the path of poetry so many years ago and
then kept me on the straight and narrow way.
Thanks as well to Poetic Matrix Press for
publishing these poems.

OUT OF THE UNDERWORLD

Exile Monologues

ANOTHER MASSACRE AND DRIVING HOME

—after Nazim Hikmet

There is lifting and lulling, circle after circle,
dark birds, a flying eddy
of loud, inch-wide mouths.
The sky undulates and slips past,
its darkening alive, a gliding-by of eels.

I never knew I loved the repetition,
the road, curve upon curve,
joint of stillness and motion.
The world is windmill, turning and oblique.
It rattles many panes of grey.

The small, live things are thick
that fall around and through the sun and stone,
nudging the momentum and the rolling.
The traveling edge inhabits us. It almost calms
with its indifference, its hum of rods and wheels.

I never knew I loved the weight,
graze of black stones at the roadside,
revolving sun that stains with light and heat,
passes and passes again, laying the dark glaze,
the years, heavy upon heavy.

I never knew I loved so many,
their unseen falling, light upon lost light.
The white sum held up without hands.
A storm to be read later, with dreams and heat
and the memory of many palms.

SOFIA

i.
Far back it is, my beginning
in its ruined stillness.

I cannot say, with words, the line
around the calm of it, the invented calm.

ii.
My children come with eyed and curving faces.
They want a story: a cycle and a resolution.

What they want is a game, a token, an hour
bright with winning, rules and spaces.

iii.
But the story is heavy, a bag that sags and pulls
through a wild light the lost and worst.

The walls that opened, the fires that fell
and made the shape of flowers.

A dusk of words that floated without meaning,
shapeless. We were pale, out among the small.

The little black nocturnal things who fear,
who tear the dark with running and burrowing.

iv.
My house touched the dark correctly, with voices, lamplight.
Then a different dark came, with fire, a shriek of noise and color.

The raven flew off with fire sounds that altered in
its bird voice, the different size of its understanding.

The black wings of the bombs took less
than the love of breakage, knowing and abstract.

Eyes with joy in the burning, and eyes turned away.
Eyes that lived in the following calm, the wilderness of calm,

And the light of forgetting that comes after.
That light is the bear that chases you.

It determines where you run.

v.
I tell my children something old: Rome full of farlight,
gone so something better could come. I lie.

Or how the universe came in a Big Bang,
making a sky of magical waves

that released like rain the blackness,
the heavy weight of being nothing.

Absolution: a hill of light, a tide
one can't resist. I lie again.

vi.
I show them my hand. My hand full of Here.
It is heavy with Now and Forgetting.

Severing the old world in its weighted cloud.
The calm of it: the palpable, imagined calm.

ANASTASIA

> —*After the Bolsheviks executed the last Russian tsar*
> *and his family, rumors arose that his youngest daughter,*
> *Anastasia, had survived. A woman called Anna Anderson*
> *claimed to be the missing Anastasia and persuaded*
> *many influential people. Anderson was a former mental*
> *patient and worker in a Polish munitions factory, who*
> *had suffered a head injury in a factory accident.*

I come from somewhere else, wielding a face
symmetrical but hanging like an apron.
Everyone is watching
this face with its left and its right,
not deft among the severed, moving truths.

Its stillness suggests an injury,
a different language, clouds of stinging bees.
Its mouth is wide in this shared and scented air
where even the dullest women are purple at the tips
and their thoughts open wildly, a springtime of declarations.

Is it possible to forget who you are—or to remember?
I want to hold and aim one sun-colored fact,
a foreground to arrange the many slant and sideways objects.
A grey weld fastened to a memory of sparks and skill.
A cold North pulling rapt blue navigators.

Some weep at my story, a pleasant background sound—
a small sound like seltzer. Not, I think, the noise
of the true bereft—the moans, the winking bullets.
Not the grimace of those who were loved and then slipped
suddenly below the world—like alligators, eyes last.

AMELIA EARHART

I observe the tallness of nothing,
my face small in the turning,
its blink of skin alive.

Still here among the scentless moons,
the island alight again in the dawn
and the lowing, butting weathers.

No animals, no whetting of tooth or ear,
but the air makes a sound of hay,
winds as hot and yellow as straw.

My world is the same today: eyes of want and rain
dry air hard as a mountain, impassible,
the paleness of chalk in my mouth.

The air of morning jumps and whirls.
thirsting like a devil, gradually
uncovering my hunger and my bones.

I bare my love of dials, tools,
ring upon silver, upward ring
aimed high in the aisle where no one passes.

Its whiteness revolves slowly
in my hand like starlight,
like water, like faith.

DAPHNE

So there is something after the gale
of feet and hands and breath,
the heart that rises a little
and utters a brown noise
like the pulsing, broken bird.

A memory of failing, which I will keep,
of falling below the line of sight
and the pale stone of his shoulder,
becoming part of its weight, loved
for my lost cry—when he remembers.

A snow of light is falling,
a hush, thin petals. So much
white that his face is gone.
The moment is still now, complete,
and the terror tall and permanent.

I am the wide shape left
like a silver, churning light
for those in the space around me.
Like honey, I fill my new height.
I know silence, I hear sounds oddly.

I am larger, twisted
far into the shadow on the ground.
I reach with a sound of leaves,
and there is no one.
I will not be human again.

PERSEPHONE

It is dark. A seeming blankness
made of too much space
or not enough.

Am I dreaming, hurt?
Has someone died
who matters like the light?

Can I bail with bowl or bucket
the height of this black-and-cold?
Can I see the moon's remembered curve?

I twist my head as if I might
have an ear full of colors or starlight.
Is there, above, a tide of rolling monsters?

Or a circular brown dusk
dry, yellow with lion,
curve after curve, eye upon eye?

I call into the unseen shape of the dark.
It is all gone—light and bird,
the disc of weather.

Oh, she must be coming
with her flying hair, voice and fingers long,
breaking the air in front of her.

Like the dream, she is under my eyelid.
Make her speak the light,
bring back quickly what is lost.

Oedipus

Everything I ran from now twists open like a flower
in an ordinary place that suddenly bares
its steepness, the blank odor in which it hid.

The road was silent in its odd, curved lines
but it was fierce and jointed like a tiger.
It bore its glowing marks with no intent.

A mark I too wore innocently, like a skin
of stars, its pattern invisible to me
but strange and beautiful to others.

I ran in fear and light
with a turning, tumbling eye.
The distance changed, and the perspective.

I entered the cold, blue canyon,
the different distance of the watchers
for whom the lesson and the loss sing.

Far from me, their fingers
will find a melody among black keys,
a sun in the forest of burning gods.

.

WHAT CAME BEFORE EXILE?

—With a nod to Dante.

What came before this?
The last right thing as I walked
between the swing of my city hands,
ignorant and without anger?

Far back it is—a moon, say,
or a stone or soap or bowl.
Some small, white weight repeating,
used like light but not quite seen.

I live now in the hills, with the dark bees
in the dreadful parable of the village.
The flying mouths and eyes that gather all
and seal the little rooms with minor meanness.

My mislaid city, you repeat the years
that speak like fire or jasmine to the memory.
The talk, the striving, hot with consequences
like the sky's recurring, burning rock.

I hear your stone and racket,
the salt, the yellow slant of light.
The hill where the pale winds protected me,
where those who loved me mattered.

How many turns until I am reconciled,
until I know home by its heat and distance,
as the blind do?

THE LINE

Around my exile is a line of green.
I had not quite reached it when the cold
came, the white sun dropping,
low and lower, its arctic stone.

I walked the space of banishment.
There was falling and shouting, then belief.
Silence that repeats and hardens
the leaf and the lost green sound.

In memory how they ache,
the old and vanished scents opening
my hands that were deft in their heat and bone,
holding the long beans, the easy, ordinary loves.

THEN I WAS HERE

One minute I was there
in all my faults, near the river,
my shadow in the sand and cool light.

A sky alive in its waves.
A wildness of trees
colors cresting on the moving water.

Whatever was wrong was far away.
I was blooming
and no one cared what I did.

Then I was here, heavy and pale
waiting like the stillness of bread.
Watched and punished. The rising canceled
and only the fear moving,

Yes, there might be clearer water here
and newer words for loss,
but I live in the other words,
old and imprecise and working.

Nothing I can say here will be heard.
What we need is a miracle,
one not too hard or hard to believe,
one that doesn't take too long.

NASTURTIUM

I'm polite in exile, backing into smallness.
My shoulders itch among the dark shapes,
the odor. I wait unlit among the strangers,
for someone at home to forget,
to stumble on the lines, to blunder.

To open for me the road home,
the red, percussive doors, the braggadocio,
the reputations built by fist and heel and elbow.
I am unsuited to this solitude, this unimportance,
where I want different, lesser things.

I want this little flower that is everywhere
common as sunlight, triangular butterflies.
I know it's just an oddity of color
beating this air that doesn't matter,
glowing on the unkempt shadows.

I have crossed a line
that makes a flower strange.
I live in a thin stem—in my eye
that is small now and has no language
but wild colors in a place of scent and shape.

ALMOST THERE

My flutter of shadow goes into the forest.
My walking is full of wind—a gait of leaves.

Everywhere is echo, mirror
of what I love and do not have.

My eye is a bloom of water and image.
Its love is slow and green, a floating insect.

A speech of shade, of paint,
of forever, almost there.

Marcus

—*after e.e. cummings*

Oh, once I had a reputation,
a tall light that glances and forgets.
Oh, the sting and the wing of it.

I cannot sing the half of it,
myself without my other self, little
voice that falls through would and was.

Oh so easy in the near and how,
and so strange over there
in the swear and scare of less.

Your Eye's Blue and Wishing Moth

MOMENT

Come to the thudding, floating window
where jointed mountains talk to distance
in the cursive colors of horses.

The mountain hangs in the sky
in its socket of white mist,
a ghost of knowing.

Anyone can put hands to this blue
lifted rock that holds the stillness,
turns the shadow and recurring moon.

You who hesitate will grieve,
will one day hold this gliding moment
like a defunct map, a dry, bent wing.

THAT PLACE

Try to hold it down,
that place that is more
than a place of the eye.

Place your boot on the directions,
the toe like a brush stroke,
the heel set down hard behind it.

Enter without token
the tangential winds.
Fasten with paints the light,

The rain in the leaf colors,
curve upon curve,
sigh over sigh.

Van Gogh

Go forward white and without wrinkle,
you of the thumping, unassuming torso.
Take your loud and tilt-eye memory,
the little, muffled axe of your heart.

The place you have is small and stiff: The wall
is strong but transient, alters like a stain.
Fold it leafwise; rest on the moving air
your eye's blue and wishing moth.

Break with lines the border leaking stillness.
Any lights you took up for their softness,
playful in their small and mild edges,
light as kittens in their flour-colored hair,

give them back. Take the wilderness,
the howling world of spine and odor.
Name with unstill paints the holes in the dark,
the wandering, haloed forests.

CÉZANNE

The one below his mountain
waits in the din of light.
He marks the elisions,
the shapes stranger,
more subtle than knowledge.

His eye is at an edge. There is no form,
no memory without this wait
above the fault of thought.
The noise of words is small, not wanted,
a rattle of agates or large-bodied insects.

There is only patience, and the light,
the size and angle of the understanding.
There is only earth and stone and here,
with an abacus of curve and straight,
to store and know the distance.

Miró

Kneel on the uphill light,
a place of winds, of spells.
A hollow, levitating light.
The eye's joyous space.

An ear, a painted bird,
a flying wheel.
The clear goes by in outbursts,
bulges in the sun.

The clear is axle, bright and sudden—spinning.
It is not like waiting, not like time that is long
and thin like the sad of a finger.
Here we ride the sing of now and light.

BRUEGEL

—The Blind Leading the Blind

With eyes that turn like daisies
they stare toward the sunrise.

Six blind men, their faces and their sticks
askew in grey, pointing up and down.

They lift a whiteness of palm
to the nearest pale shoulder and begin to move.

The day's hot circle is over them.
It tugs them forward with confusing warmth.

They who also move in the moonlight
that pulls the water and the fish.

Fish the color of brushing and biting.
Many darks with creatures in their wake.

Do they know redemption lies in water and a fall,
a pour of tepid starlight on the soft, slow snow?

THE NUB ON THE AXE OF THE WORLD

—Response to Robert Hudson's sculpture, "Books of Wood"

I sit on the grey of the world as it moves,
the color of wood rubbed in moonlight.
The mass of the world sliding
forward and downward.

There is balance in the blow that seals everything
with edge and weight. The cut that ignores
the fragrant apples and the loud, blue birds,
that leaves behind a wail of white.

I think I appear only once—here,
in this light like a fall of silver nails
I fill myself with the dying, spotted world,
the knocking of the pale horses.

I, the stub with eyes, riding it all,
hand-wide, sentient, shining like a jar.
I tilt on the brevity, the hour ringing
the tight circle of my shape and time.

Will the arc release me at its end,
to rise slowly like a light with handles?
Will I fall like a pile of rocks?
Will I make a noise?

Will I go gladly like the waterfall
sliding off the tall rock, gaining speed?
Will something stay, my eye that is
high and calm and heavy with the world?

EMPTY

First, place your intentions on the corners
like stones to hold the opened space,
objects flapping wild edges,
bird sound in the flying papers.
Then make a sky that fastens them to stillness.

The beginning is a hole,
as sentient as wick or brush,
a mouth from which to lift or fold the real.
The square, completed, holds it open,
this emptiness full of light.

It is plane to hold the height of number,
to bear colors, words, and weights.
The white canvas rolls in the world
until it is smooth. Until it is full
of odor and mixed with sun.

NARCISSUS

I cannot look at you—or anyone.
My sister is dead, who wore my face.
The gods who loved me are angry.

The cornice of my days has fallen,
the light and dark go everywhere,
the colors sideways like winds.

The sky is loud in its waves, the blue gone.
But my face floats in the small pond
where my eyes are upward.

I don't see beauty there, but nearness to the dark.
I see its rocking outline bleed or breathe,
its exhalation of black birds.

My stillness is a cave where some darks move
like ferns, and some are deep and sharp as reefs.
And there is only one clear face as silent as a light.

SIREN SEARCHING

The ball of light is in my eye again
grows full and rattles like a dial.
I tap with a foot the white and quiet rock,
the loud, black sea, this swirl of time.

I am dark at the edge and wasting
for one more beautiful than I.
I am a vertigo of shine and shadow
long among those sounds alive as wolves.

Will I find him or die searching still?
Will I love as I dream the floating images—
invading again with my ear against the circles,
the red, receding hooves of the sun.

I lean always toward the listener.
As I dance with his distance, my feet sing.
They turn like moons, they are white,
they burn in the whirling bright.

In my hands, dark will tilt and wail upward,
eat the glowing air from everywhere,
hurl light, a storm of snow and birds. I die
of my lengthening hands and their sky-full of song.

Around me floats my sound, repeating,
a beat like a gambler slapping down
a lamp-lit sum of number and a color,
and that strange echo that is beauty.

SOMETHING HALF-SEEN

The eye is trained by what it catches sideways.
A flash, a flag of eye or elbow
in the old god's cannibal mouth
or one live shoulder clarified
by angle of sea or labyrinth.

The space slants in and out
on hinges of light and strangeness,
speaks in the calipers of dream
of something lost and ripe below the image:
an unknown ore, a devil, or a magic spring.

A woman walks thin by thinner
into the green of a painting's shade,
leaving the empty shapes of her steps.
Her smallness is built of continuing,
walking the eloquent light of the image.

This opening speaks to the sleeping eye
in its bone cave, its black marrow.
There's a spot in the eye where much is caught.
The dreaming eye that touches all
with its oiled, loosened, knowing glove.

EASTER ISLAND HEADS

What was it like to wait without rain
or leaf among the silent truths?
To stand listing in the winds' chalks
the many smallnesses of dust?

Black granite gods, tall and taller
in the light as final as a mountain:
The powder of vision is on you, dry waves
of colors, the lost whirling of the builders.

Is it good to remember all the reds and blues
that fasten for a moment like the tides?
To breathe the light like an animal
beautiful in your sorrow and your duration?

"CRAZY OTTO"

Otto paints his house again,
with his changing love of colors.

The blue and green are high with hopsack edges,
the stops of yellow clear and low.

As if something is recited and a mark made
where each mistake is swallowed by another.

Each daub taller, brighter than his eye or word,
his loud and undistinguished singing.

No one color ever reaches
the sky-colored end of the job.

Someday, one color, one light
uniting all the eyes.

OTHERWORLD

SANCTUARY

They boom in this tall, indifferent place:
those moon-colored nights
like water in a long white ravel of river.

To see them you must pass the edge,
throbbing animals that run on curves of claw,
moaning, lifting their dark mouths skyward.

You must pass the human words,
the church of territory, with weights
and workers, a black house for kneeling.

Must disregard the theory and its preacher:
the gloved and inauthentic rumor,
acrobatic names for how you came to be here.

Hear the cold apartness growling, the ice,
the white pole keening indecipherable light,
the loud sky rolling out illegible stars.

The stars pour over the indifferent shapes
a water full of scars and red lights. Wear them
as if they were warm to you, and do not kneel there.

EXPLORER

In his chest a red ship skids and thuds.
He arrives with a scrape of wood
at the new and unintended vision.
Error lifts the bright hairs on his skin.

His eye veers, here among the green
dimensions. His wish for a wick of road.
There must be a forward somewhere
in the tall, wet, unspent curves of rock.

His map makes a noise like wings,
a bird-high wind of law and prayer: A hope
that the size of the accident just might
excite the queen as much as being right.

She owns this wilderness of lights now,
he says as he bows toward God or goodness:
Bellowing suns without a fixed location
and a heat appreciated best from far away.

He will harden here among the rocks,
the fire-colored veins. Look up and shake a gravel
of bright stars over his story. Scar with his tools
whatever is near and gleaming and unsafe.

JUNGLE

The heat is dark and the soil dark
where all directions bloom.
Faces look everywhere, bright as hinges.
Pale breaths hang like cloths.

The petals here rise sharply,
sing their scent with wide, white beaks.
The odor of flower roots
on any fallen stick.

Strangers stop in the rankness of "now,"
the clotted light that sees them.
The sky is wet and heavy like the stones,
thick-rooted minerals, pockets of oils.

There are no limits.
They are rich.
All that they are
will blossom.

MAKE OF LESS

Hear the mutter in the bone,
joints guttural and stingy.
Renounce the far, high places
that you grabbed with eye and tendon.

Make of less a grand complexity,
an explanation long and branching
of objects to avoid or reconcile.
An elaboration not far from simplicity.

See in dream the stopped wood filled
with creatures, eyes the color of spoon
near enough to jangle the metal blood.
Do not go there by the real moon.

Learn to be the throbbing background,
the odd light of a corner, near to dark.

WHERE THE OLDEST GODS LIVED

Dark rock and cold, bright water.
Edges of great height, large lines
where sky and shadow move.

Nothing that implies the things
alert and toothed and tilted at the eye,
little warm cries with large, absurd intentions.

No way to foretell the change
that will dull the rocks
with a callus of creatures.

No animal to eat things smaller
and more beautiful than itself.
Nothing that flees or tricks or dies

among the thoughtlessly strong.
Nothing yet that moves the gods to exit,
Making a racket of angry water over black rock.

The old gods see the sky come down
to those alive and temporary, dragging its particles,
making its gradual case for blue or gray or cold.

The gods behold their journey toward smallness,
their odd wish to watch the mortal and accidental,
to want the foolish awe, the alteration.

BRIGID

—Brigid was a goddess of sky and weather in pre-Christian Ireland, the patron of poetry and early spring. Her festival day, Imbolc, was a time to predict weather. She invented keening, a mourning mix of weeping and singing, and a whistle for night travel.

i.
We land with a magic whistle,
small and ignorant
at the bottom of the night sky:
the animal hour alive in all its furs.

Sky in its purse of rain is heavy, black.
Even the land we see by day
is the weighted land of words,
bouldered, carved, and hard.

We put our ears against a vastness.
We, the dumbstruck, see
all the tricks and cracks of light,
downpour's iron bell that swings the dark.

ii.
We come to storm or flower
as we must: wild, untuned.
We pray to stars and weathers:
to all that turns in the dark.

We crave the gentle goddess
complicit in our music and our mourning.
She who makes the equinox with traveling
birds and the candle-bright spring rain.

44

She who keens, in her height, our loves,
our losses, the demons that we dream.
She folds the sky for us,
absolves the numerous and small.

We hold her travels like an unkempt song:
her weathers, her poets' curving apples
picked from tall fires
with our long and grieving hands.

DEATH CARD

You cannot see him in the world.
Look instead for those who slow around him:
His tap of blue-white poison
loosening the body's inks.

Look at his picture thick with edge:
hood, blade, blackness. They say it means change.
The dark in it comes of the confusion,
the cries and falling around the change.

The change itself is just a moment,
the cut abstract and painless, a shadow.
It is powder, a soft fluttering.
It curves in air, a flare of moth.

See how he holds the hearts that come,
all of them laboring, bumping like camels.
The surprised, who arrive bad-tempered, spitting,
speaking only the language of heat and burdens.

So many: misshapen, beautiful, vicious.
Most come slow to the transformation,
touching both the shadow and the earth.
He widens just a little as he waits.

HIGH PRIESTESS

—a tarot card

Narrow by narrow she rides.
Woman with a tall blue ball on her head
and a horn and another horn
and a no eye and a why eye
and a new moon through her dress.

To see her you must live in a jar
or a rock or an alphabet
or a planet balanced on a dark.
On a "why" of seed and stem and under
and made of wide by wide.

You must see white to white,
your heart stem paling at the leaf.
Face of chalk and torso hard as tooth.
In the high-low, pile moonlight silent as sand.
Release the cold and falling salt of judgment.

MAGICIAN

—a tarot card

At the tall of his head a joint of ovals.
At the long of his waist a sliding snake.
His robe goes into the brim of the dark,
white and sentient, root-cool.

He is thin as a candle, yellow at the hair,
and unfolds in his long, clear hands
the casual edges of the middle,
the carnival of changing forms.

One hand up and one hand down.
A sky that alters like a rose
where goes, ribbon-smooth,
his eye and his taller, wilder palm.

There is a wand, a rattle of lines.
A big trick, loud and loved by children.
His face like the candle and the flower
leans away from the quiet shadow.

His face of curving shapes
ambiguous among the changes,
yearning forward, almost symmetrical
like the markings of hounds.

HANGING MAN

—a tarot card

Why is he still and smiling?
And why is he beautiful,
dangling by the thin of an ankle
into a tree-high yellow day?

The mild man is upside-down,
one leg straight,
one with shadow at the knee,
his head bottom-up in the dayshine.

How fixed his yellow rim of patience,
stopped sun or eye of wolf,
a light as bold as marigold,
real to the thumb as coin or corn.

His hands behind his back insist,
touch a hidden shape,
the pause, upright and thin,
before the hard and winnowing climb.

He knows in the steeps of why and sad.
At the keen of where and when, he knows.
With weights of eye and smile, he knows
the near of "now" and "not."

THE LOVERS

—a tarot card

It is different here: the first man and woman
naked, colorless, their feet tangled in stillness.
And there is no wind or water
where the choice is made.

No meaning is hidden with darkness
but all is painted in odd glyphs.
Around the first ones are trees in all their colors.
More colors than the spread of your fingers.

Tree of fruit and snake,
tree of fire burning upward.
Voices they imagine.
And shapes, a mountain and a cloud.

They cannot see the red and purple angel,
a sun above him, colors on his hands.
His hair is leaf or fire,
a flying of red and green into the light.

They cannot hear knowledge, his billow of vowels.
They call upon the words they know—not many.
Only an ignorant choice can,
with pain and time, paint them wise.

STAR

—a tarot card

See the stars in the daylight sky,
everywhere the points of shine,
bent at a shape of water.

A woman with star-colored hair
is in the light of yellow and white.
She has no shadow. She gathers air

and water with her bowls' bright rings.
Her foot rests on the river without weight or sinking.
Around her, starlight moves and pours.

It matters like the water in her hands.
And it seems that she has always been here,
in someone's dream of innocence.

She and the dreamer both
breathe the colors of her window,
the light already and always open.

In some dark elsewhere lies the sweating mine,
the war. She will never see them
and the dreamer wants it so.

In this window, only the odd clarity:
star and water, dazzle of yellow flower,
the little scarlet bird alive in its edges.

Symbolic Animals

Monsters fold in ink and the wind of the story.
Their gaits swing and utter.
Not nailed or lidded, they wander.

They make a forest, a skull full of stillness,
revise with wands of shape our ignorant eyes.
They howl the horizon's size and ability to move.

In grins the color of moon
they shake us in the magic.
Behind them stands the hero:

Well-shaped, distracting, the dumb assistant
near the magic spotlight, the sidekick
disappearing, oddly bent, or cut in half.

These creatures don't live on the road,
the straight black line that any fool might follow.
They own the edges deep and rippling.

They conjure a dark singing,
bring an undulation
like the fire or river we stare into.

We watch them with something under our skin,
a reverie or festering joy,
the Other as it flies or slithers.

In every day that loosens beauty like a poppy,
they twist and roll an eye more yellow and more fixed.
They love, those lying, dreaming, jolting shapes.

PURGATORY
(AFTER DANTE)

LEAVING HELL

i.
The wailing dark is gone,
the punisher's slick face
hot and shining like a boil.
The distance is landfall,
a climbing motion, a seizing of rock.
The abyss still throbs, but not here.

Hell is now below and far away,
a shadow, a cold, black wave
that changes and repeats the losses.
In my fist, the prize of forgetfulness.
It is odorous and bulbous, human,
waiting on the loud white rock of morning.

ii.
Above my eyes, the air is cold
with the moonlight I will climb,
the round, white silence of dream.
The day holds the windy eagle,
wheeling a song, a prayer, a cry
that folds it all in a pale circle.

My first dream is a dream of flying.
The battering wing comes down, the claw,
the lifting blow as blue as flood.
Between my foot and the ground, the air
moves and I might fall into the pale dust
like a seething of hoof strikes, but instead I fly.

iii.
I land in the moment over the mountain
resounding with the falling of rock,
the turning faces of the climbers. The rising

of accords, difficult, sinuous music.
Some ultimate silver chord
that chimes and spills me over.

The polished gate, the colored steps,
the brightness turning like a wheel,
the brilliant waxen angel clothed in ash.
He tilts my forehead like a map,
writes the errors I must climb. I,
who ply a mountain with my mute foot.

GATE

With a white-boned wrist,
a veer of colored eye,
the dying touch
a pane of nothing as they leave,
keening the smooth and window-colored rain.

They who remember living—
the skin, the ardent muscle, the waning
bones that speak to moonlight
with their pitted color—
they wish to go on gently, unmolested.

When they come to judgment, they are loud
in their protest, their flailing bags of hair and skin.
Entering the ribbed and vaulted dark,
the difficult climb on leaning rocks,
each dying torso is shaken.

But now they are here. They are higher.
They face the eloquence of gate and key,
the angel hooked and muscular
with wings like a loud surf lifting,
and a face that frowns and knows, twisting like an ear.

Angel, let them through.
Let the soft glyphs of their footsoles
read the rocks as they climb.
Let them bear the writing on the forehead,
the sad white stone of what they are not.

Let them through
with their memory of eyes.
The light the eye can carry
in its hanging, unkempt purse
is as nimble as a pulse.

Prayers of Iintercession

*—Dante encounters souls in Purgatory who see his shadow
and realize that he is not dead. They ask him to seek prayers
from the living when he returns to the world, to shorten their
time in Purgatory.*

i.
This is a pious, climbing place
tall in its hat of yellow light
and subject to the winds of intercession.

You come upon a broken dawn.
It is hard.
It is crockery among the shadows.

They are here,
in the steep place that gathers
those once powerful on earth.

They come to you,
those pale souls, eye-first,
mottled and beating like clocks.

They see, and don't see,
your white and frightened breaths
that rise like small balloons.

They call and prod
demand the coin of prayer
with voices that rattle like old wheels.

ii.
There is another and more urgent air,
a tangent sky as clean as flint.
A dream with a blue window
or just a blue view in a window.

Its weight is around you
as if you are known to blue,
as if you had swum in blue
for a long, wide way.

It is taller, smoother than the night sky,
that black and other wave
finned with silver swimming,
with leaping and soaring and sounding.

It rolls and buoys in blue light, in its own
time: the unintended intercession,
the beauty that wants nothing,
that doesn't even know you are there.

CLEAN

*—The souls in Purgatory can only climb toward the light
in Paradise during the daylight hours. If they try to climb at
night, they will fall back to the beginning of the climb. And
the climbers carry the stones of their mistakes on their backs.*

Shadow covers the mountain of atonement,
covers the sinners carrying their stones.
From the swaying horizon
rolls a dusk the color of elephant.

Night stops the rivers and the climbers, stops
the many on the earth who pull at the net—
or the seam or the root,
the little task that bends and binds them.

Night stops the scholar bowed and grey
above his page of rotting words. He sighs
like a housewife moving a gritty cloth,
an alkaline, disfavored wish for clarity.

They all thirst for the slow, white dawn,
the right and gradual word
pulled glowing like a tusk
from the world's blue, enormous shadow.

They want to wake at the end of the climb,
at the shining motion of river
that wipes all longing with its empty color.
To drink at the horizon weightless as a flower.

CLIMBING AT NIGHT

The climbing penitents
fall back into night, repeating
the first Fall into the world.

Above, they glimpse the resolution,
a far thing fragrant as a garden,
a sorrowing of mint.

They carry in memory the first ones
who disobeyed, who fell into life
and went on with their crooked thoughts.

Who labored with their limping tools
in daylight, pulling a rocky shadow
through the bent and livid vegetables.

These climbers see, like children, the first tree.
They put the thought of tree near the thought of moon
to turn the silver light, to see what is bowed and full of gravity.

The night climb is an error they can measure:
the weight, the slowing beats, the loss of height.
An error they can straighten by surviving.

NIGHT IN PURGATORY

Night means something here
where the dead reoccur
between a mountain and a starred sky.

Where stars mark the end of Hell,
with a higher burning: lit and angled stones.
Where all on the slope look crookedly.

They go lopsided up the mountain,
on a memory of eye and heel,
breathe a strange air bent by meaning.

They must stop sharply in the pointed night,
the dark that touches them like thorns.
Must accustom themselves to the heaviness of stars,

Must master the footing of climbing,
and the different rising of dream, apart
from the jointed metaphor of the body.

They remember their time on earth
where, deep in its color of leather,
their brown eyes searched the rocks,

Foretelling the small, dry branches,
usual in that latitude
and loud in the wind as sparrows.

The mind remembers the tall planets,
their colors singing a language of light
and distance and flying not spoken in Florence.

The eye remembers being lost, a marsh
overtaken by the strange blue lights and the damp,
the soft muds and their varicose paths.

They remember and go on, barter the grey rocks
of their errors for the difficult, empty circles of sight
Atonement they will carry toward the stars.

SNAKE

*—The saved souls waiting to begin their climb through
Purgatory reenact the temptation in the Garden of Eden. In this
ritual, the outcome changes and the snake is driven away.*

These newly dead, having been all—
child, and wrong, and long in the world—
come again upon the source:
the painted snake, circle-shape that slides,
forward on its urgent ring of words.

"No, not for you the slow, sorrowing climb,
wearing the dull stone on your back.
Love the error in your eye. Let it take you deeper
like a root-white muscle that is brighter
after blood and fighting, fleeing or dancing."

Having been all, the dead allow the words
to loosen, like leaves, their yellow faces,
their breaths that slide among the tree-shapes.
They sigh the lost, round ache of blood,
the muscles long as rain. The wild wishing.

Then, they lean once more upon the mountain,
the hard climb on the silver breath of the rock.

ANGRY

Call out the banging that you know,
the sentries loosened like beaks.
You, roiling in your ecstasy of anger,
dance in its color, its smell.

Your air rolls with fog and smoke.
It is black with anger,
the color of hole or shadow.
Your air holds much and holds it long.

Is there anywhere an end of anger
a tall door distant as a city in a light?
A window slant with voices
that swing out like torches?

Can you find it by the hazy ways
you know with a darkened ear and foot,
the shift in thickness or steepness?
Do you still speak to radiance and morning?

LOVE

Yes, yes, it is loved,
but it's not the right thing. Or it is
the right thing, a blooming, wild light,
but I love it in the wrong way,
too much or not enough.

How hard it is to see the lines
in the middle of joy. Is it wrong
to call the roses into light,
to lift up red or yellow like a horn?
Is it pride, is it gluttony, is it lust?

Love bends without thinking
toward the ripening petals
wide and sideways on the stems.
A color dropping into every space
as if it is heavy. But it's not, it's just right.

It's light, and I don't need your atonement,
with all its mountain of falling and failing,
its sighs of loss and dark.
It dies of lines and penance,
kills this color and this scent of rising.

LOVE RECONSIDERED

Cup, eye, and swimming cell: So many circles
with a trailing breath of want and matter.
And love, like the windmill of light-spotted sky
turns heat and color toward the small,
the faulty in their freckled skins.

One object fills us, coming from the side,
again and again, like a flicker of bird
until our faces turn and we breathe
it in like the wind or weather
as if we always heard it, always knew.

Lent like the cup or the sound in the flute,
a round, wild dream of grace:
The one we love with our moving,
all our whorls and circles,
our music like a river of blue spells.

LOSING VIRGIL

He told you he would have to go,
the guide who flew and rode monsters,
lifted you with the knotted length of his arms.

The one made by the gods of his time
and barred by the later, larger god
who came with your ladder of Light.

The one who took you without envy
to the flying angels, looking
with bird-wide eyes into your moment.

THE MOUNTAIN ROARS

—Mt. Purgatorio shakes and roars with joy when a penitent completes his atonement and ascends to Heaven.

It is more than the tissue of air,
the revelations coming, color by silent color,
to those with light on their faces.

More than a border marked
by a door, a stair, or gliding secret
in a green and weightless dusk.

There is stillness. Those at the final gate
look up, having expiated all,
rest their feet on the last shadow.

There is sound. The mountain moves
its loud and interlocking rocks,
booms as they leave time.

Its height sings everywhere,
in the dark and knowing cracks,
the white wing and fall of water.

It knows, the mountain that hurt them with images,
that shook the heaped, imperfect hinges
of their bones and their beliefs.

It roars joy as they climb past the metaphor:
the shape of mountain and atonement,
the always-leaning castle,

The tall first hour as a human.

LIGHT THAT PURIFIES

The light that purifies is not a cold
and tactile thing. Not held in the bend of fingers,
and not in the small and folded senses.

It's not bright rain that weights
with a little, intermittent width
the sleeve or leaf or roof point.

The light that comes to the garden
when it's too late for innocence
burns and stays, a windy roar of lead.

It tears wide the dusty mind and skin.
It does not answer to the curious,
insolent finger or the tongue.

FIRE

*—Dante walks on a ledge adjacent to fire. He must pass
through the fire before he can enter Paradise and see Beatrice
again. He is afraid, and his guide Virgil must urge him
forward.*

i.
Fear is close around me,
like the noise of my clothing.
The wicks of sense are moving,
a roil of small openings.

I come to the fire,
not as the talented pilgrim,
but as the animal that walks behind
a nose and eye and tongue.

Between the fire and the wind
I lift one foot on the little ledge.
The edge where memory stutters,
tangles love and word in a wish of snow.

With closed eyes and a skin,
I sing the song of the fire:
the swaying city, the wolf,
the glove of small, cruel instruments.

Fear is orchestra; it lies between
silence and every sound at once.
And it is home to the soft
fern-wide sounds not yet imagined.

ii.
Is it gentle on the other side?
Is there more than eye and skin
and their accidental pangs—
my own eye in its house of lid and bone?

71

Will it still my hand — like a stone
the color of deepest water?
Will it move my eye like the speckled dove?
Will it quiet my face with shade?

Will it make of me a calm and different knowing,
a cool grey shining far away,
singing to the round and dappled earth
with its slant of oval rain?

THE RIVERS

> —*Near the end of Dante's journey through Purgatory, just before he sees Beatrice again, he meets another beautiful woman picking flowers beside a river. She bathes him in the rivers Lethe and Eunoe: forgetting and remembering.*

Two waters: forgetting and remembering.
The first a sigh of petals, white smoke, air—
as if the way to Home were soft.
Then, the memories as sharp as drowning.

Two women hear him near the portal,
bearing his purple, gulping heart,
its chambers of eel
applying themselves to Home.

First the woman with flowers
singing the wide of her mouth.
She washes the inexact and root-white man,
in the river's immaculate motion.

And then she drowns him in remembering:
Every good he saw and slighted,
every grey and sliding misstep in the world
and its waters dark with stone and carp.

He sees the Other through the water,
what is light and door for him:
That woman tall and distant
as the small, exacting rose of the moon.

With the water and light of her eye, she measures.
The world returns with all its windows: He sees again
the colored forest, its flowers, hawk-quick shadows
and all the paths for being green and lost.

Not innocence but a seeing long in its root.

Thirst for Light

SUNFLOWERS

Here is the narrow hour in its furrow:
now, before, and after.
The row longing at the end of the light.

Petals wide over wide, edge over edge,
flowers loose in their weights, so much yellow fastened,
swaying, at the bottom of a blue and drifting sky.

Above, the taller, rounder air,
with its bell of stars, so many turning rims,
a rolling, burning wilderness of circles.

Praisers, raise like jars
the small, crude rings of eye and word.
Garish, unsubtle, clear as coins.

DECEMBER DAYLIGHT

Dreamt or painted somewhere else,
the small sun gleams and gutters
in the grey light, gaining like a pearl.

The shadows move,
lengthen weightless colors
close to the eye and leaning their stems.

Darkening like old bones
the slants of tall and jointed grasses.
Drops on edges brighten and then move.

Each pulls down a single light
a curved, reversed image
a color twisting.

Only dream or distance holds
the assent to the turning,
the cold, grey love for small light.

THIRST FOR STARLIGHT

None so small
as those who err
and wait, faces up,
under the many colors of stars.

Waiting there for goodness
or a purer light.
An answer in the night sky
colder and higher than hands.

Are they dry or are they water, those stars
uneven in their moving edges,
shining like salt,
revolving in the dark like snow?

Is there even something lost and comic
in a light that folds and flitters?
A beetle upside-down in silver,
waving filaments of shine.

No science of starlight
so bright, so tall
as the strange and thirsting distance,
the night in its pulse of white rain.

SMOKE

Angled like the waves
are extinct lovers
who utter time and distance
with a silver light.

Their breaths still rise
distinct as ions, commemorate
their thoughtless pulsing—
 thoughtless only in the moment.

They are the grey dissolving opal
at the tip of the flame,
smoke undulant with stone and fish-scale.

They lift the weight and shine
not wholly seen
but gathering everything.

The space
between burning and nothing.

GOAT'S EYE

—*Predators have vertical or round pupils. A goat's pupil is a horizontal bar that moves, enabling the goat to see far from side to side. The devil is often depicted with goat-like eyes, and separating goats from sheep is metaphor for parting the saved and damned.*

i.
Two curves, above and below,
with hair and skin and shadow
compose the mild, unblessed eye.

Two colors: wet and yellow coin
black line flat and moving,
the thin of dark coming under a door.

Goat goes into the light.
Light goes into eye,
turns the wheeling pupil.

It makes a short wide world of
wolf and pointed grasses. No
dazzle of light above.

ii.
You, predator, turn and slide
your glances, your round eye
with its small black dot.

Part those others from the saved.
From strangeness make your demon
hoofed and horned and oddly eyed.

Swing without thought
your bone-full teeth that sing,
your jaw of words reciting a tall light.

Lift your voice as if it knows
those wild, indifferent suns
that say nothing of being blessed.

ASCENSION

Mark your arrival by the ache,
your burning breath. Mark it
by a guard, a password and a gate,
an unusual woman on the other side.

Imagine it as height,
a view that you can earn
by rising, growing stronger
like a light or a voice.

As if rising were the rule,
the Word, the Book
with the writhing illustrations
that make it hard and steep.

Where to go but up and sparse
in the climb that takes everything:
All that is sized to human eyes,
all that is merely good.

THE LOVED

Love shapes the one loved
with the white, awed silence on its hands.
It does not lift the wide and faulty
to its narrow eye.

Does not admit
the common or the small
when sun makes sharp the till
on the bright edge of a face.

Oh, love is brighter than a water spider
rare and blue and sunlit on a skin of image.
It is thin and long in its stepping,
a shimmer of stepping.

The loved is quiet in a bead of light,
is a stillness of glass.
Is loved without banging or breakage.
Is loved only.

Dark

The dark opens
like a bird or a refrain,
makes loud the forest.

They speak in calls and whistles
who come to the unfamiliar dark:
The death apart from speech.

They gather the meaning
not with tooth or voice or claw,
but with a savage wonder.

The light is small and subtle
that moves in the branching dark
like finch or aspen leaf.

BEAR AND DEVIL

Think of a devil.
Think of a bear.
Each one with its still weight
upon a curve of stone
and turning at the eye.

Then they lean into the world,
the song of prey or conquest.
They do a sudden dance of strand and bone,
elastic in the thought of motion,
the dense and gleeful muscle.

How far they will dance
from where they start
So much is mauled in their stepping,
under the winding constellations.

They sway and pivot,
spiral under the starlight.
Their strength spins heavily
a machine, wild and newborn,
a rolling of notch and tooth.

BELIEVER'S CANDLE

Believer, make a candle.
Make it crude and bright as you,
short and thick and beating like a hoof.

The world needs dark about it
to make it stay and mean, and
loud, round lights to hold like badges.

So lift the lights that burn,
love the moths that drop
and shake black noise against the skin.

Believer, come scalded with a death, expulsion.
Come starved to water and your wish for water.
Come all the way to a sad and knowing wish to continue.

Lord, love this believer in his failing wax.
his world that softens and deceives
if you hold to it a light too gentle or too long.

OUT OF THE UNDERWORLD

From a place of hands and blindness
the seekers come,
small and crouching like furniture.

They touch the little beaded lights
clustered in minor roundnesses
and leaning like cobs.

They call for the windows
that bring a strong, bright wind
and long blue rugs unrolling.

They call for a body unimpeded in a white, clean sky.
But their bones still hurt in the maze of sight
as if the gods of dark are heavy and are here.

There is nothing to mark, with a sharp light,
the edge of what they lost to dark
and what is simple and can be gathered.

They have reached a dimension of number, rolling,
gears and axles loud, unspeakable, repeating—
an arrival not, after all, a place to see

but a bowl of wild music, swerves of sound and meaning.
Wall and angle do not mar their seeking.
It's the melody, the lovely, strange gradation.

About the Author

Patricia Nelson is a retired attorney and environmentalist. She has worked with the "Activist" group of poets in California for many years. The group rose to prominence in the 1940s and 50s and is now undergoing a resurgence of publication by a different generation of poets. The Activist credo is that every word in a poem should be poetically "active," employing some kind of focused poetic technique—a principle not as self-evident as it might sound. The group often works with metaphoric imagery.